No Place Like It

Hugh O'Donnell

DOGHOUSE

No Place Like It
is published by
DOGHOUSE
P.O. Box 312
Tralee G.P.O.
Co. Kerry
Ireland

TEL: +353 (0)66 7137547
www.doghousebooks.ie   email: doghouse312@eircom.net

© Hugh O'Donnell, April 2010

ISBN 978-0-9565280-0-1

Edited for DOGHOUSE by Noel King

Cover illustration: Beth O'Halloran – No Place Like It
www.bethohalloran.com

The publisher and poet thank
Dublin City Council
for its grant for this volume.

Dublin City
Baile Átha Cliath

Further copies available at €12, postage free, from the
above address, cheques etc. payable to DOGHOUSE also
PAYPAL - www.paypal.com to
doghousepaypal@eircom.net

Doghouse is a non-profit taking company, aiming to publish the
best of literary works by Irish born, or Irish resident, writers.
Donations are welcome and will be acknowledged on this page.
For our 2010 publications thanks to:
                    Kerry Education Service

KERRY
EDUCATION
SERVICE
Seirbhís Oideachais Chiarraí

Pr

inted by Tralee Printing Works, Monavalley Industrial Estate, Tralee.

for
Michael Moran
1949 - 2009

rainbow –
seven flavours
of rain

Acknowledgements are due to the editors of the following where some of these poems have appeared:

Cyphers; Gold: Laois Creative Writing Anthology, 2008; The Irish Press; The Natterer; Poetry Ireland Review; Revival; Salmon: A Journey in Poetry,1981–2007; Shamrock Haiku Journal; The ShOp; Southword; The Stony Thursday Book,No.7; Studies.

The poem, *Endhouse, Gordon's Bay* was short-listed for the Strokestown Poetry Competition, 2008.

'rainbow' was voted joint-best haiku by readers of Shamrock Haiku Journal for 2009.

Special thanks

to Beth O'Halloran for the cover image,

to Noel King, editor of Doghouse,

to Jack Gilligan, former Arts Officer, Dublin City Council and to Sinéad Connolly, present Arts Officer, Dublin City Council,

and to Anne-Marie Glasheen, Liam Ryan, Eileen Sheehan and Barbara Smith for their proof-reading.

Contents

One

Two

One

The Pedestrian Zone

Pacing the pavement like a biped
strutting your stuff – head forward,
the pained face of a crumpled flower –
you meet others dragging a leg
or swinging a cane, practising.
Along the street, mothers hold infants
in their arms to see how it's done;
soon they'll be taking up
where grandparents left off.

Not long ago it was tree-hopping
and singing love songs to the moon.
This morning it's clear you are here
to perfect your walk, to purchase
some street-cred with your own peculiar
dodge and shimmy. Couldn't be
simpler: placing one foot in front
of another for as long as you live
until you can do it in your sleep.

Complaints Section, City Hall

Dog-shit on the pavement
means our eyes falling shy of a neighbour's
So what are we looking at?

Railings chipped from constant rattling
of stick against taut strings. Pigeons...
Between the bars inspect weeds.

Our building site. The crane, mechanical heron,
mostly still. Officials pointing out the invisible
Sense of purpose in the air.

Swimming pool please with a wall of noise
and a playground for new mums to visit
Offer them a second traffic warden.

Children out late, living off fluorescent sweets,
gum, nicotine, beer...
Two gardaí strolling in the dark should suffice.

Add in druggies, shootings, sirens,
knives... dog-shit on both sides...
Look interested, don't forget to smile.

A Few Hard Knocks

1. No matter what, stand up to the day
2. Take the kids out. Warn. Rebuke
3. Batter them with words of misspelt love
4. Rinse your mouth out. Spit
5. Allow for the sucker punch
6. Inhale. Recover. Avoid the mirror
7. From the Pro Cathedral a bell rings and
8. he's there, handsome in a white, silk scarf
9. In the corner, getting dressed, it isn't all that clear
10. just how good you are.

Rules of the Road

Just wait 'til she gets him home, this four-year-old,
flaming-haired boy who has just walked out
in front of a car and she on the kerb
with a child in the buggy, losing her mind.

You little bastard, she cries, dying
to get her hands on him, to tear him apart
as he retreats from what is not a playground,
whimpering at her madness and tears,

at her cursing him from a height, threatening
to teach him the lesson every boy must learn
about breaking his mother's heart by crossing
the street, taking his life in his hands.

Between Stations

Just now we could be anywhere
along time's spine,
the sun through wide windows,
a woman un-papering a sweet for her friend,
both sucking as they notice the furze has caught fire
and some fields are growing sheep.

In the seat behind, a child
composes plaintive sounds, bleatings –
will he ever learn to speak?
his mother sighs. *In due course,*
she says repeatedly, *in due course I said,*
raising her voice to quieten him.

War Babies

On the hour you can have a car chase
courtesy of Sky, good quality shots from the front,
strapped bodies taken from the house, the leftovers
of a family feud. Then the small change:
accidental shootings, baby snatches, tribal beatings,
a Presidential address from the White House.

Afterwards, you spread out a map of South East Asia
and count the islands or ask your father to explain
the history of the world just one more time
before the searchlights sweep you up
between the prison wall and the perimeter fence
in a yellow jumpsuit with your hands tied.

The Curate's Boy

Later on, he might wonder, what was it like
to have watched a father dress up
in all that finery, soot of soutane, biretta, lace,
and proceed with small steps to the altar –

to have listened as he rambled on about Abraham,
Moses and the Good Thief: how they prevailed
while bodies piled up on some street corner
and the looting began – or when the sickened

called up their sins and desired his signature
on the air, what was it like to be standing by
with the holy water as the old lady searched
for another breath and found one?

Batwatch
Natural History Museum

It looked like an alien, unable to struggle
out of its parachute, to the girls
from St. Mary's, chittering in the quiet,
notebook in hand as they stood by
Plecotus Auritus – the pricked ears regal,
wide eyes pleading, *break the glass,*

undo the pins. I have no business here.
In another story, they could have been
children on their way from Sunday school
trapping frogs whose bodies they would nail,
ankle and wrist, to little crosses
while the boy with a pellet gun closed an eye.

House Rules

The Godfather's old school pal squeals to the police –
the one who's claustrophobic –
for which he is strapped into a life-size box alive ...

Keep an eye, my grandfather said to his little girl
while he slipped out of the shop 'on business'.
Don't draw them on us, warned my father.

Every day the undertaker wakens early:
breadwinner with an air, having loitered
over the threshold – remains, removal, remorse –

unlike those grown-ups who sidestep and fumble
when it comes to shutting out the sun,
watching their backs, trusting no one.

A Little Terror

1. Hit Man

Travels light; change of underwear,
a second shirt, toiletries, nail clippers –
always keep your hands in mint condition
(motherly advice) – Panadol for migraine
or a touch of sinusitis, pen with extra cartridge
of ink, a new blade, earphones
for late night listening, white handkerchief,
an Agatha Christie for unusual delays,
street map, shoe polish, surgical gloves,
bag of boiled sweets, a naggin of whiskey,
clean overalls and all to fit neatly
in an old brown case (his father's)
the one he always packs for luck.

2. Scene of the Crime

This is the house where they planned it
over three days, with no one leaving
until he had chapter and verse by heart.

This the wall where questions were asked,
where a bungler's face was re-worked
with a blunt instrument. Here's the brick

(red) that was used to finish him off.
Forensics can detect the hair and tissue
but cannot hear the force of his appeal –

the bus was late, I dropped the key,
I hadn't dressed for rain – to a man
who could split a brick with his bare hands.

3. Interview

They offer you a chair – tubular
legs, short back – to ground you,
to bring up your sense of self,
sense of occasion –

like being at Granny's
and sitting still or at the dentist's
from where you give an account
of some predatory lapse.

You are plainly a sitter, safe
in the hands of a child who rubs
your plasticine self into shape
while you purr, squirm, miaow.

4. Chamber Music

The song and dance man
follows a strict routine.
When he frowns your body
thrills like a plucked string.

He snaps and you sing
your heart out to comfort him
(face down, heels in the air) –
but he is beyond comforting.

Whistleblower

He had long hair that was greying,
held a paper sword that he waved
at passers-by who didn't laugh
when his weapon blunted and the daft
look heightened in his eyes. In his cap
the coins amounted to little; small drops
of rain quietened him. Inside the church
a bank of candles glowed and smoked.
He could temper his blade there, compose
himself, lunge, startle his own shadow.

The Elder Son

Treat your brother well.
Invite him to your table,
have the best wine accompany
a hearty stew. Converse,
spend time on a crossword's
difficult clue. Enquire
about his wife, offer a post-
prandial mint, cigar, liqueur.

Rather call in the experts
who know how to vanish him
down a black hole
only a cockroach creeps out of.
When you stop noticing
his shadow on the wall
count to ten,
say he's gone missing again.

Bone of my Bone

Neanderthal, our oldest, coldest case
despite the best of us - forensic style,
nurse in white apron wondering what
crossed your mind at first light;
did you call out *Day* or sigh,
raise your arms to be lifted, you,
half-sister, our family secret,
(a little slow so sent away to school).

Yet times when weather pits itself
against our being here, I sense the chil-
blained hands and feet, small cries,
lullabies before spring arrived too late
and you had disappeared,
leaving only bone for us to study
your posture, profile, pedigree,
your alphabet, humanity.

Home From Home

The other occupant has just vacated the kitchen.
I can hear him downstairs dropping his empties
in the bin. Moon-time steadies him.

Nothing unusual really, just trust dovetailing:
in that way avoiding manoeuvrings on the stairs,
eye contact, the need for subterfuge

as one only enters when the other leaves
to a tap dripping (its double drip), the air vent
moaning, a red light flashing on the phone.

Migrant

It is, after all, a job to the man
who stands on a mound of stones
with a hammer in his hand.

He has been at it for hours,
chipping bits of concrete from cobbles
then tossing them in a bag

for the next collection. At intervals,
the yellow dump truck arrives, bleeping
in reverse, and pours out another load

to keep him occupied. Mostly he sits
in his orange vest and hard hat
like a penitent in a prison yard,

tapping for all he's worth, but
when he straightens and climbs the hill
for a better view of somewhere else

he is David with a slingshot,
Sisyphus in a dream of ease,
a farm boy shutting out the farm.

Endhouse, Gordon's Bay

Washed out my body lies in weed and grass
in all the places where we once did pass.
                    Ingrid Jonker, Escape

Morning and evening we unlock then lock
the length of chain across the driveway –
not that we've seen anything suspicious.
                    *

The juice from the crushed berries by the gate
sticks to our shoes and makes a mess inside.
Avoid them. It's not our house.
                    *

At night the sea insists on a big presence
and covers us with the sweepings of the floor.
So far down, we dream and dream.
                    *

That red stain across the water you noticed
on the way to Hermanus is not shark food.
I've made enquiries. It has a name.
                    *

Evenings, taking the path through gnarled trees
to the restaurant, listen – a man persuading a woman,
laughter round a fire, wave-fall, backwash.
                    *

This close to the edge
we feel inclined to put down the book and undress;
to swim out with no thought of return.

Hurricane Miranda

The folks who live on the hill
          sung by Peggie Lee

The worst part is this: that the forecast is
always so nearly right – the storm
stirring itself, having heard plinkings
of music from afar and now making straight
for their arms raised in protest...
and prayer matters so abominably, *please,*
there are children, but it blows across
the playground tossing swings in the air ...

These are the stories that end happily
where they add 'a wing or two', rebuilding
shattered lives in patched-up centres
with someone paid to listen as they tell
of Jack and Jill who lay together
one summer night on a beach and woke
to this howling, who couldn't climb
high enough, never rose to a house on a hill.

Last Resident

Between showers (and shutters) a rinsed-out light
seeps in, climbs the wardrobe and finds
an unused kettle on the top, the handle
with a strip of shadow down one side,
a length of wire dangling. From bed level
walls doze, the mirror looks in mourning,
the dressing table's bric à brac gone into dark.

It's possible the kettle could remain up there
at least until the lease runs out – the building
already earmarked for better things.
But this afternoon as thunder crumbles over,
is it any wonder she feels moved to squander
what she has for something else, less scary,
as she opens up, flushing in the day.

Quartet

1. Afternoon Tea at 'La Petite Tarte'

A faint black line across her back,
she chops the fruit, or is it veg?
her body rhythmic as she grates a lemon.

At a guess, she's thinking carrot cake:
more likely, what she'll wear this evening
going out. Beyond her, that someone

might be tempted to return next day
to ease a v-shaped piece from the cake-
stand, take it and eat.

2. Greengrocer

At eight, she arrived and opened up.
The garage door slid open on a greased runner
letting out the dark.

The first child in asked for spuds,
a head of cabbage, an onion.
The red arrow quivered on the scale.

Eight-thirty, someone cut an artery
in her neck. The blood ran
out the shop and took the incline fast.

3. Getting Away from it All

So she checks in with an out-of-work clown
the girl with a limp
from a punishment beating

who just wants to squeeze into
a swimsuit, paint her face
and snuggle up to the sun.

There are jokers in Iraq, he chides,
splitting their sides
and having the last laugh.

4. Party Girl

Despite the crunch of glass underfoot,
wine stains on the tablecloth,
she never wants it to end.

Only losers leave early, she decides,
those who'd never understand why
strung out on stars, she carries on

with some unlikely Solomon,
all travel and baby-talk,
his camels down on their knees outside.

Stolen Car

5.45 a.m.
                    a new car is being introduced
              to the neighbourhood
something held in check released as engine noise
                    as urge to outlaw the predictable
     zebra lines of walkways boxed-in clearways
                    self-care in a carwash
     rousing her to loosen up her early morning
bouncing over ramps while the police are stopping off
                    for croissants and coffee
     shrieking with the sudden change of direction
                    mounting the path
steaming down to the end of the cul-de-sac
                    out of her mind
     safe in the sweaty hands of a fourteen-year-old
                    braking in a shudder
              ashamed to think of herself
only turning right when the filter arrow blinks
          spring-green   cruising   changing down
                    nosing into the driveway
the handbrake jerked   up tight

Eden Lite

No dogs, no snakes, no nudity,
just tourists from Chad to the Azores
sprawled under the cherry
blowing pink night over them
with park attendants, litter bins and clouds
which pull over and park right
in the sun's eye and nobody says *boo*.
When it's sunny the office girls audition
for a part, hiding out in designer shades;
in the cool, they drift away like that woman
with a bump under her coat being warned,
get that out of here or I'll call the police.
Lock-up, it all falls into place with a little ragging.
Grass lies back, trees open up.

Flying Lufthansa

Our French attendant is trilingual.
Without a word he holds you with a look
which says, *terms and conditions may apply,*
or, with some sourness, *no hurry, madam,*
we still have twelve hours of flight-time ahead.
As needs be, he will insult, harangue, serve,
address, enquire, compose, insist.
In effect, will ensure that order is maintained,
cabin fever averted, a singsong arranged,
should it be necessary, with everyone joining in.
If you protest, you will find him man enough
to fling yourself, your child and duty-free bag
out over Africa – *au revoir, bye-bye.*
His position absolute, he will happily go down
with a charming reserve, advising passengers
to tighten their seat belts one last time. Tightly.

After the Play

Crossing the bridge she looks down,
it's been painted since we went in
to that dreadful play.

I have learned not to demur at revelations
on this scale. *How do you mean?*
On our way over, she says, *it had a matt finish,*

now it's a high gloss.
See for yourself, those reflections,
how orange and yellow spill inconsolably

across. Forgetting myself,
I try to explain how nightfall
might account for the illusion

before she stops and takes my sleeve.
Have you ever listened to yourself?
You should just listen to yourself!

Anam Cara

Soul-friend with a dozen cautions, I know you
on CCTV, know you with my coat fastened, a box
of Milk Tray and something for your mother, know
you magnified, a life-size dream coming towards me,
know you fading away saying, *it's too cold for snow,*
know you when I lie down, get up, your voice
on the phone though you cannot pronounce my name...

but not your footprints from the shower, don't know
your acid tongue, blood type, your crumbs on the table,
your congealing silence, don't know where your body lets
you down, times you stand out in rain and scream
or laugh in a way that's not quite laughing, don't
know what I really want to know about you – maybe
what's left over when it's over... hands? nails?

Eileen Gray at Collins Barracks Museum, Dublin

come into the parlour...

The idea of it; lancing a tear of lacquer
from the rhus and holding up a shell,
as one might, for a drop of the oozing

Christ. So agile her mind playing on
a lacquered screen, lantern, dressing table,
lightweight chair, on this living space

drawn into being as if awaiting
our dawdle through her rooms, suitors
who desire to be uplifted, held, approved.

Kaluso Trio in St Mary's, Tuam

I can see three things,
A game, a scorning, and an earnestness
                          Julian of Norwich

Distinction consoles
so someone has to leave the performance,
her kind of coughing disallowed.

Tut-tut, tut-tut sound her heels to the healthy,
those well-wrapped for the damp space
God's word needs to thrive. A blonde

cellist opens up and savages the strings.
More strings please. The violin hurries in.
Behind them the pianist needs watching.

Game over. Downpour of applause.
Three heads bowed.
Now where was I?

Taking Stock in Station House, Attanagh

Just three taps on the lightstand
brings on full light. There are four digits
(our family secret) that control the alarm.
Our gate doesn't close fully, it tightens up
halfway home. Two clocks continue
at loggerheads in the front bedroom,
each one insisting, *I said it first*. One
cat keeps the garden free of mice
and the dangling feeder mostly full.
Three strikes and you're out
if the gas doesn't light.
There are five of us between seven rooms.
There used to be six (but who's counting?).
One tap for dim, two for semi-bright.

Curriculum Vitae

September, maternal anxieties conclude
this has to be the break in heartbreak
as First Year daughters answer
the come-on of conversation, sons
fumble with each other, or slouch
by the wall, prematurely grey.

Later, in Elizabeth's herb garden
we take a leaf between our fingers
and sniff, then talk of Lucian Freud,
how seeing his nudes makes us feel,
the body brought to that telltale,
prescription ripeness where it spoils.

Magic at Coole

In Coole Park, Elizabeth is first to notice them
sixty or so metres off, an elderly man and woman
linked by an arm but stalled, half-turned, unsure
of themselves; have they walked out too far?
Would going on be wise? They appear on the edge
where definition blurs and the light through beech
dapples – an effect Cézanne creates for his old
seated gardener, building for him much-needed rest,
sifting his figure in sunlight. Down a woodland path
this vision of love, of frailty around a cane and now
someone wanting a photograph. In that moment
they turn away, as we would wish them to, back
into themselves, the weight of her arm over his.

Old Love

The pull and drag of a train out of Connolly
takes five seconds to pass,
seeding the interval as surely as bird call or church bell,

reviving some sleeping sense of keepsake
I must not neglect,
to know her as life pulse, as reason to get along.

Two

Crèmerie Restaurant Polidor, Paris, Photo 1912

In the middle, the owner, mid-career, left hand held
at an angle, the right hidden in a pocket.
Hanging back, his wife perhaps, luxuriant hair
piled up, posing, her shoulder to the jamb,
hand to her face, the fingers of the other spread
on her hip. Two solemn children out front, boots,
coats, hats, one six say, one eleven. Behind them
a waitress, patterned blouse, long skirt, wide belt.
Left of her, four waiters in aprons, white towel,
dickie bow, waistcoat, one's hands by his sides,
another's joined in front, the poise of men who
know how to serve, approach a table, engage.
Close to the owner, two chefs in white could pass
for comedians with their baker's floppy hats,
anxious to get inside, camera shy, their three hands
which are visible closed in a fist. Beside them,
stands a man in a dark apron, trusted with supplies
maybe, his place secure in an improving business.
In the corner a small dog has entered the frame.
Twelve people on the street fronting the restaurant,
the dark interior like the future behind them.

Table Manners

On entering, someone will go down
on his knees and examine the floor
in a prolonged bow after which the gong
can be sounded by the one responsible

though not before the all-clear has been given
by the kneeling scout, his heart skittish
as he inspects teeth marks
where the lino has been chewed

and checks a small hole in the skirting.
So the men sit down after grace,
their talk of politics, genetics
and who will draw the short straw.

Round the table their white and balding heads
turn slowly, *how good to see you: how long it's been.*

This evening memory sifts for the good stuff,
yarns, characters, one-liners, small epics

in which they shone before the recent warfare –
mild stroke, routine procedure, a stent slipped in.

Constitutional

Some day I will follow your peak cap
sauntering above the crowds
                              and notice
how it lingers by a statue of some saintly friar
as you cross the main street, read the name,
catch his eye;
                    fall in as you make your way
towards the grim river, intent, masterful
in a frail kind of way,
                              lose you
as you slip between buildings or stall
at a doorway font, dipping your fingers
for safe passage.
                         Later, you'll turn out
your bag – apples, bread, milk –
                                        the rest,
what can't be shown, frittered away
getting from A to B, from here to there.

The Cure

I

Must and a dangling cobweb in the room,
the missing teeth gaping in welcome.
Like tobacco in his palm he kneads the pain,
his head at an arthritic tilt,
hands you a bottle then to seal recovery,
waives the stipend until you heal.

Behind him the part-time girl
drops a cube of sugar in her cup and stirs,
manoeuvres her wedding ring.
There's little hope her body seems to say
as if returning to your door the scabby mutt
you dumped miles from home.

II

Hot breath on the ear, *he's having chemo*
(familiar form). Of course everyone
of a certain age gets a blast of it sooner
or later. Later, give or take
a spot or two, recovery is intoned
as though the key had been found

and turned until another scan, a second
course advised and you're left facing
his wide eyes pleading, *tell me,*
to the child in you who sits out break-
time in the corridor for not knowing
where the limits are, nor wanting to.

To the Nurses' Station

take a left at the portrait then straight on

That's him – looks like a banker
or the founder of a charitable institution
with the sanctimonious smile of having
found the elusive antidote
or made his millions on soap.

Above the navy blazer, background
for his joined hands, full of knuckles,
and a tie that blinks on and off,
beams the reassuring embrace that takes in
how lost and poorly-dressed you are,

how careless your hygiene, how
furtive your entrance, how pathetic
the gormless grin you spill
as she lays a hand along your arm
and enquires, *who let you in*?

Into Your Hands

Blood-tests, then the slow burn
of waiting for results. Then hearing
without listening, rummaging
among the offending words
for the 'all-clear'. Time to begin
the prayer, *please God, don't
let it be*, to count your blessings,
consider the lilies of the field.

Since your last visit,
you have found yourself filling
your brush with skylight, lingering
for hours in Connemara weather
simply to stall in the way
you'd press your hand down
on the polished table for the imprint
and its disappearance over and over.

The worst of it. After a while
there's no draught flowing through.
A door slams, conversation ebbs,
words being unhelpful servants
in the end. Neighbours knock less
and seem enviably busy as they pass.
When they do, nothing they say
comes even close though you smile.

It might be tempting to write about
the hospital instead of the car park;
easier to step the long corridor
to the sick room, to lash out
and yet – the strange comfort
of jaundiced walls at midnight,
baby cars in their cots,
the rattle of small change in the tray.

How you wanted to take his hand
and bow down, to befriend him,
tell him how gifted he was
like the leper the Evangelist drew
so well having him leap and swan
and swallow before the miracle –
he did it; he really did –
breaking his promise not to tell.

Miracle

Was he ever here? asks mother
as an afterthought (meaning my father)
and we sift through the evidence.

After her check-up, she sits him down,
God bless your hands doctor, then,
lighter than cherry blossom,

she drifts from the Eye and Ear
having seen for herself at first hand
what no eye has seen.

Days Like This

There are days you feel blessed
at another's achievement – his eventual rise
to a post, her reaching across you
to accept the winner's cheque, his clearance
at the doctor's and not yours,
her credentials lauded, his position kept,
yours closed, her smile the one
that clinches it, his hand gripping yours,
meaning, 'don't let it get to you',
her sly wave from the windswept window
as she turns back to her desk
and glances at him, his youthfulness trumping
your under-used years,
her fullness, his aftershave, her pension,
his voice on radio, her strings
in the string quartet, his son playing rugby,
her daughter following Mum –
blessed for no reason but that this late April
the doctor has allowed you home
for the long weekend and it's raining outside.

Elegy for Michael

I
Salt

You weren't well that rainy afternoon
we drove to the Museum of Country Life
in Castlebar to see the meteorites

and the leftovers from another age
where we browsed imagining the creak
of wicker, a shower of stones.

Even then we couldn't know
you were beginning to disappear
into what you would leave behind –

mandolin, brushes, watercolours, flute –
what your fingers had played over
long enough to call your own. But

it is the rest we miss; the clearing mist
of your laugh, salt grains on the table
and what you would make of it all.

II
School Attendance, Gola

Imagine it. We'd head out early,
you with pad, pencil, small box of paints
and twenty Major wrapped in cellophane.

It should be perfect as we glide across:
the island virginal, empty houses staring
into themselves as we pass on

to where the old school sits on the edge.
High tide must have caused a fuss on the step,
we agree, the teacher putting down the chalk

to listen and go on listening
in roofless rooms – rusted coat hooks
by the door, the window space forever painted in.

You take a seat outside and start a cigarette.
I leave you be to question a ghost-child
about the others and what became of them.

Reliquary

Last night I consulted my dying father;
I'm worried about you, he said.
He had seen me fumbling on the floor
having dropped the precious relics
meant for him which broke and scattered.
He could tell I was wondering how am I
going to put them together so that Anthony
is really Anthony, the Little Flower
her true self, the splinter of the Cross not
some dusty look-alike; with trouble ahead
trying to return them to the donors
who could probably tell their original
from a fake, know first class from second best,
notice a scratch they hadn't seen before,
who would soon be testing a fragment of bone
on the next sick heart, cancer rout, trickle
in a brain and expecting results. His back
was skeletal when I moved in and touched him.

Garden Shed, Faversham

Special because yours, this narrow strip
of grass, narrower path to the shed
where ivy clings with a drowning man's embrace.

Inside, dampness housed, space to straighten
a nail, shave a piece of wood you found,
discover what might go with what.

Perhaps we have it wrong and you come back
to inspect your makeshift mower, to stand
corrected, cut string for the rose, details

we hardly notice as you mend the wooden door
to your world with a recycled nail or screw,
self-satisfied, *now that should do*!

The Trick of Passing Away

First, his hands turning diaphanous,
threadlike and swarmy as mist
disappearing up his sleeves.
Then the face, that too, starting to thaw,
to wriggle off the bone
but the whole head already leaving
the way a woman might leave the room
in distress, her face held in a piece of cloth,
her body following
until there remained only the pink tie and shirt,
beige jacket, flannels,
all crumpled now, shapeless, flat, ill-fitting.
Finally the moment we didn't know
we were waiting for
as one black shoe fell over on its side
then the other.

Planning an Afterlife
in memory of Joe Lucey, Salesian priest

Breaking-in is not necessary, the door pushed back
to a space awaiting the touch of a child's hand
to startle it into life. Unlikely now as dust,
noting the vacancy, arrives and settles
on the Mother and Child from Indonesia
(freed from a hardwood), on a lost St. Francis
with his unmasked, clown-face, on a stack
of CDs full of Eastern chants. Still, wouldn't hear

of trying to transport sandalwood-scented walls
elsewhere, the room tallied to the last fingerprint,
hoisted, then reassembled alongside Mr. Bacon's
dream-stalled studio in the Municipal.
So choose; pot plant, figurine, rain stick, oils,
a poster which says, 'let me know when to go
and when to stay,' the creaky laundry basket.
Let his dwelling place be broken up, scattered

in small allotments as memories, what remains
flung from a third storey window into the street.
Better that way than keep a shrine without a breath,
without water running at times, a phone answered,
a clink, a cry, a crash. Invite then the arsonists.
Let there be sirens, theatre and ladders to the sky.
Let the children gather, a neighbour take a beer
from the fridge, snap it open, lift up his head.

Carpe Diem

There is nothing you can hold on to –
certainly not the latest news
which can seep away in an hour,
not the afternoon with its bouquet
starting to fade, not the tree on fire
with green light, not the friend
you just made in a coffee shop
while asking directions, not your car
inadvertently parked on a clearway,
not your parents' generation,
not wisdom, not your ego, not soul;
not a sentence with its airborne
syllables nor a story whose beginning
and end don't gel; not God
whose hands are forever soapy,
not the water in the sink, food
in the fridge, not your wounds,
healings, disgrace, not advice,
not even the line that begins,
'there is nothing you can hold onto –'

The Golden Mean
for Iggy McGovern

Meaning what?
the failed mathematician in me enquires,
that it all adds up?

That a formula exists like a handprint
on the oval ball of the earth
with its gardens and goldfish,

seating beneath the stars,
(every hair numbered, tear tagged),
showing where the hand has been?

Harvest Festival

Flown in specially for the season
of squashy fruit, designer-dark,
she keeps it light (world hunger)
as there are people to be thanked –

whoever dressed the church, draped
the pulpit with ivy, made the scones
and tea and dear Lucy Boyd
on whom Christ could depend his life.

So we sing our way down to the last
verse of the last hymn then drift out
to handclasp, compliment, frost
on the tongue. Behind us headstones

loom, the dead retreating from the front,
in the hall a jostling towards the spout.

Gatekeeper of the Dead
at ease in the fellowship of the afterdeath
                              Chris Zithulele Mann

He keeps to his chosen circle by the gate,
a path worn deep by his endless shuffling
or stands by a half-door looking out
at those who stroll in the garden, recalling
mortgages, forest walks, fast-food
joints, money they thought they had.

It was only done for a laugh when he applied,
but after the final appeal and phone call,
he comes to, knowing the chaplain lied –
no party girls, no after hours. The hate mail
still comes from the other side to which he replies
with the standard, *no regrets and no apologies*.

Snow at Fiumicino

Lulled by its miniature through a skylight,
we sit halfway down a stairway
in the airport, counting
the cancelled flights and wondering
have we enough money for another night.

Later, we vigil to the souls of all who have died
in airports, poisoned by coffee
or by excuses wrapped in cellophane.
We lie on the floor in our travelling clothes,
the seats already draped with sprawling bodies.

Despite the hour, a community of nuns
continue to lead spiritual lives in an upright position
while an African manages to draw
the wrong kind of attention by attempting to sleep
in comfort under the huge globe of Leonardo.

The next day we take off, burnt-out and bearded,
until, ears popping, we land at Zurich and recover
in the glare of resurrection, the chock-a-block of Alps.
We are afraid to applaud for the memory
is fresh: but we do, discreetly.

The Long Room, Trinity

When time is short,
let the museum suffice
for a sense of narrative,
What went before? What next?
or the gallery for reassurance
that this is the business
and your ten minutes adequate –

but for the sweet smell of now,
the library: here drop off
child and shopping at the door
and breathe woodland,
your whole life clarified
for what it is – scribbles on a leaf,
guesswork, first go at a plan.

Christmas Eve, Syngefield

Invite me again, John, to stand in the doorway
to see the robin eat porridge oats
from your ungloved hand or, failing that,
let's visit the young oak wood where we'll greet
Dead Man's Fingers and *Candle Snuff*
and you'll pronounce *stigmella splendidissimella*
with some delight as we inspect a bramble leaf
to chart the little fellow's progress.

Róisín should be here shortly, you'll oblige,
and she'll arrive with news from town
of trolley gridlock, the aisles jam-packed.
We'll feast then on such conversation as befits
the season, sipping, for old time's sake,
an obligatory port. Christiaan will join in,
singing along to music he's overheard
as daylight, our perfect host, tops up the glass.

Hugh O'Donnell was born in Dublin in 1951. His first collection, *Roman Pines at Berkeley*, appeared from Salmon Poetry in 1990; his second, *Planting a Mouth,* from Doghouse in 2007. In 2006 he graduated with an MA in Ecology and Religion from the University of Wales (Lampeter) out of which grew *Eucharist and the Living Earth* (Columba, 2007), a book of ecological theology.

He lives with the Salesian community in Dublin city where he ministers in the local parish.

Also available from DOGHOUSE:

Heart of Kerry – an anthology of writing from performers at
Poet's Corner, Harty's Bar, Tralee 1992-2003

Song of the Midnight Fox – Eileen Sheehan

Loose Head & Other Stories – Tommy Frank O'Connor

Both Sides Now – Peter Keane

Shadows Bloom / Scáthanna Faoi Bhláth – haiku by John W.
Sexton,

translations into Irish by Gabriel Rosenstock

FINGERPRINTS (On Canvas) – Karen O'Connor

Vortex – John W. Sexton

Apples In Winter – Liam Aungier

The Waiting Room – Margaret Galvin

I Met A Man... – Gabriel Rosenstock

The DOGHOUSE book of Ballad Poems

The Moon's Daughter – Marion Moynihan

Whales Off The Coast Of My Bed – Margaret O'Shea

PULSE - Writings on Sliabh Luachra – Tommy Frank O'Connor

A Bone In My Throat – Catherine Ann Cullen

Morning At Mount Ring – Anatoly Kudryavitsky

Lifetimes – Folklore from Kerry

pto

Every DOGHOUSE book costs €12, postage free, to anywhere
in the world (& other known planets). Cheques, Postal Orders
(or any legal method) payable to DOGHOUSE, also PAYPAL
(www.paypal.com) to doghousepaypal@eircom.net

*"Buy a full set of DOGHOUSE books, in time they will be collectors'
items"* - Gabriel Fitzmaurice, April 12, 2005.

DOGHOUSE, P.O. Box 312, Tralee G.P.O., Tralee,Co. Kerry,
Ireland
                    tel + 353 6671 37547
email doghouse312@eircom.net   www.doghousebooks.ie